# A CINEMATIC HISTORY of HORROR

www.raintreepublishers.co.uk
Visit our website to find out more information about Raintree books.

To order:
☎ Phone 44 (0) 1865 888113
📄 Send a fax to 44 (0) 1865 314091
💻 Visit the Raintree bookshop at www.raintreepublishers.co.uk to browse our catalogue and order online.

A CINEMATIC HISTORY OF HORROR
was produced by

**David West 🏃 Children's Books**

7 Princeton Court
55 Felsham Road
London SW15 1AZ

*Designer:* Gary Jeffrey
*Editor:* Rowan Lawton
*Picture Research:* Gail Bushnell

*First published in Great Britain by*
Raintree, Halley Court, Jordan Hill, Oxford OX2 8EJ, part of Harcourt Education. Raintree is a registered trademark of Harcourt Education Ltd.

08 07 06 05
10 9 8 7 6 5 4 3 2 1

ISBN 1 844 21083 9

British Library Cataloguing in Publication Data

Wilshin, Mark
A cinematic history of horror
1.Horror films - History and criticism - Juvenile literature
I.Title
791.4'36164

*Printed and bound in* China

PHOTO CREDITS :

Abbreviations: t-top, m-middle, b-bottom, r-right, l-left, c-centre.

cover, l, CINEMARQUE-FILM FUTURES/NEW WORLD / THE KOBAL COLLECTION, c, STRIKE ENTERTAINMENT/NEW AMSTERDAM / THE KOBAL COLLECTION / GIBSON, MICHAEL, r, UNIVERSAL / THE KOBAL COLLECTION; 3, Photo By C.DIMENSION/EVERETT / REX FEATURES ; 4l, 4r, Photo By SNAP / REX FEATURES; 5, Photo By SNAP / REX FEATURES ; 6l, DECLA-BIOSCOP / THE KOBAL COLLECTION, 6-7, Photo By SNAP / REX FEATURES; 7t, MGM / THE KOBAL COLLECTION, 7m, 7b, Photo By EVERETT COLLECTION / REX FEATURES; 8t, UFA / THE KOBAL COLLECTION, 8b, Photo By EVERETT COLLECTION / REX FEATURES, 8r, UNIVERSAL / THE KOBAL COLLECTION; 9t, UNIVERSAL / THE KOBAL COLLECTION, 9b, UNIVERSAL / THE KOBAL COLLECTION / HAMSHERE, KEITH; 10l, Photo By EVERETT COLLECTION / REX FEATURES, 10r, Photo By SNAP / REX FEATURES; 11l, Photo By EVERETT COLLECTION / REX FEATURES, 11r, THE KOBAL COLLECTION / NEW LINE / TALAMON, BRUCE, 11b, Photo By EVERETT COLLECTION / REX FEATURES; 12t, ALLIED ARTISTS / THE KOBAL COLLECTION, 12l, Photo By C.WARNER BR/EVERETT / REX FEATURES, 12r, Photo By EVERETT COLLECTION / REX FEATURES; 13t, THE KOBAL COLLECTION / COLUMBIA, 13l, STRIKE ENTERTAINMENT/NEW AMSTERDAM / THE KOBAL COLLECTION / GIBSON, MICHAEL, 13r, Photo By 20THC.FOX/EVERETT / REX FEATURES; 14t, Photo By EVERETT COLLECTION / REX FEATURES, 14b, Photo By SNAP / Rex Features; 15t, Photo By EVERETT COLLECTION / REX FEATURES, 15m, HOLLYWOOD PICTURES / THE KOBAL COLLECTION, 15l, UNIVERSAL / THE KOBAL COLLECTION, 15r, RKO / THE KOBAL COLLECTION; 16t, PARAMOUNT / THE KOBAL COLLECTION, 16b, POLYGRAM/UNIVERSAL / THE KOBAL COLLECTION; 17t, 20TH CENTURY FOX / THE KOBAL COLLECTION, 17b, UNIVERSAL / THE KOBAL COLLECTION; 18b, Photo By EVERETT COLLECTION / REX FEATURES, 18l, COLUMBIA / THE KOBAL COLLECTION, 18r, UNION-CAROLCO INT/TRI STAR / THE KOBAL COLLECTION; 19l, DINO DE LAURENTIIS / THE KOBAL COLLECTION, 19r, Photo By EVERETT COLLECTION / REX FEATURES; 20l, 20r, Photo By EVERETT COLLECTION / REX FEATURES, 20-21c, MGM/SLA ENTERTAINMENT / THE KOBAL COLLECTION; 21t, Photo By C.BUENAVIST/EVERETT / REX FEATURES, 21b, Photo By EVERETT COLLECTION / REX FEATURES; 22t, UNIVERSAL / THE KOBAL COLLECTION, 22l, FILM VENTURES INT / THE KOBAL COLLECTION, 22r, Photo By FOTOS INTERNATIONAL / REX FEATURES; 23t, 20TH CENTURY FOX / THE KOBAL COLLECTION, 23b, DENIS CAMERON / REX FEATURES; 24t, PARAMOUNT / THE KOBAL COLLECTION, 24l, Photo By C.WISC HIST/EVERETT / REX FEATURES, 24b, Photo By EVERETT COLLECTION / REX FEATURES; 25t, Photo By SNAP / REX FEATURES, 25l, Photo By EVERETT COLLECTION / REX FEATURES, 25r, Photo By C.WARNER BR/EVERETT / REX FEATURES; 26t, VORTEX-HENKEL-HOOPER/BRYANSTON / THE KOBAL COLLECTION, 26b, FALCON INTERNATIONAL / THE KOBAL COLLECTION; 27t, 27b, Photo By EVERETT COLLECTION / REX FEATURES, 27r, THE KOBAL COLLECTION; 28t, 28br, Photo By EVERETT COLLECTION / REX FEATURES, 28bl, Photo By C.20THC.FOX/EVERETT / REX FEATURES; 29t, ARTISAN PICS / THE KOBAL COLLECTION, 29l, Photo By EVERETT COLLECTION / REX FEATURES, 29r, DREAMWORKS LLC / THE KOBAL COLLECTION / MORTON, MERRICK; 30l, UNIVERSAL / THE KOBAL COLLECTION, 30r, Photo By EVERETT COLLECTION / REX FEATURES, 30b, Photos By REX FEATURES

Every effort has been made to contact copyright holders of any material reproduced in this book. Any omissions will be rectified in subsequent printings if notice is given to the publishers.

*An explanation of difficult words can be found in the glossary on page 31.*

# A CINEMATIC HISTORY OF HORROR

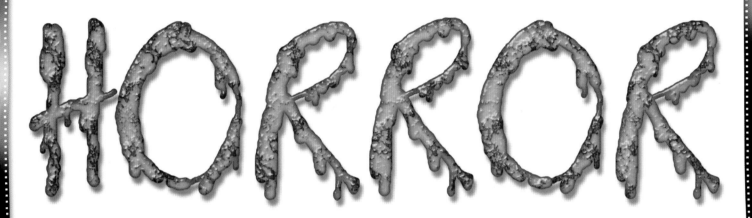

## MARK WILSHIN

Raintree

# CONTENTS

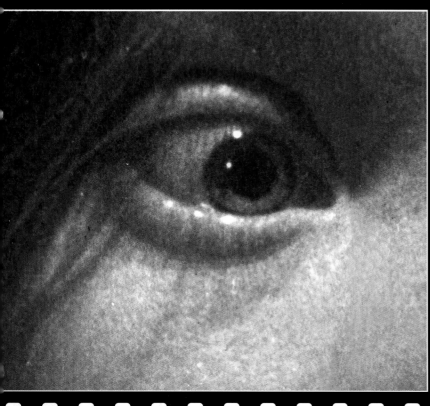

# INTRODUCTION

Bloodsucking vampires, flesh-eating zombies, and evil monsters have tortured (and delighted) cinemagoers since the dawn of film. Rooted in European folklore and **Gothic** novels, the horror film developed its own style with Universal Studios' chillers of the 1930s, creating the ultimate symbols of monster horror, Frankenstein *and* Dracula *(both 1931). Inspired by the monster movies of the 1950s and* **psychological** *thrillers, the horror film focused on crazed serial killers, reaching a blood-curdling climax with the* **slasher films** *of the early 1980s. Whether it involves sitting in the dark, screaming at bodies coming back to life, or shrieking at shadows creeping along hallways of old dark houses, the horror film is a twisted pleasure. Left peering through our fingers, we are scared by what we see and terrified by what we are left to imagine.*

# MADMEN AND FREAKS

*With vampires, devils, and mad doctors, **silent film** experimented with different ways of terrifying audiences. But in the cinema after World War I, images of freaks and deformed humans were the most horrific.*

## IT'S ALIVE!

The horror film was born with French director Georges Méliès' *The Devil's Castle* (1896), when a bat swoops into an eerie castle and transforms into the Devil. But Méliès was more interested in the fantastic than the frightening, and it wasn't until *The Cabinet of Dr Caligari* (1920) that the shock of horror became a pleasure all by itself.

## THE PHANTOM OF THE OPERA (1925)

*Viewers fainted at the sight of Lon Chaney's make-up at the première of The Phantom of the Opera. Designed to look like a skull, he used fish skin to tilt his nose, and cotton to build up his cheeks.*

## GERMAN EXPRESSIONISM

*Expressionist films created a tormented world to reflect the mind of a madman. With its crooked streets and houses, eerie lighting, and excessive make-up, every scene is full of mystery and horror.*

## THE CABINET OF DR CALIGARI (1920)

*Director Wiene's horror classic tells the story of Caligari, a mad doctor, and his fairground attraction, the fortune-telling sleepwalker Cesare. When Cesare predicts the death of a man, later found murdered, and his fiancée is abducted, Cesare and Caligari are the prime suspects. Cesare dies escaping and Caligari is tracked to a mental asylum, where he appears to be in charge. The grotesquely twisted sets are unconventional, with long dark shadows painted on the walls and Caligari's abrupt movements exposing his tortured soul. Reflecting Germany in a period of social and economic chaos, The Cabinet of Dr Caligari is Wiene's outcry against a weak German government.*

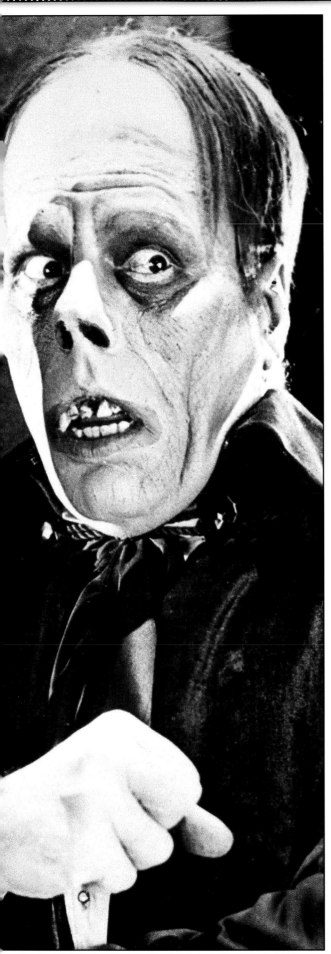

# SOUTHERN GOTHIC

*The Phantom of the Opera* (1925) and *The Hunchback of Notre Dame* (1939) were the first

## FREAKS (1932)

*Starring real-life circus performers, Freaks creates sympathy for the deformed entertainers, before they take their horrific revenge on a woman who tries to exploit one of them.*

steps towards a distinct horror style. Using **gothic** settings like the towers of Notre Dame Cathedral in Paris and the labyrinth of tunnels, lakes, and crypts beneath the Paris Opera House, these silent horror films were full of dread. Yet despite the monsters' horrific deformities, their tortured souls touched the hearts of audiences.

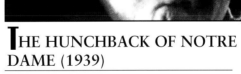

## THE HUNCHBACK OF NOTRE DAME (1939)

*Charles Laughton made the monster, Quasimodo, in* The Hunchback of Notre Dame *truly pathetic as the obedient servant to a mad master.*

## CARRIE (1976)

*Based on Stephen King's novel, Carrie has the mental power to move objects from a distance. When she is bullied at school, she uses her power to exact revenge.*

# MONSTERS AND MUMMIES

## THE GOLEM (1920)

*Based on Jewish legend, the Golem is a clay statue brought to life to protect Jewish people. One of the first screen monsters, the Golem helped to inspire Frankenstein's brainless power.*

*Combining the distorted sets and lighting effects of **German Expressionism** with the **gothic** atmosphere of horror novels, the Hollywood studio, Universal brought lasting horror icons to life with the disfigured monster and the embalmed mummy.*

## UNIVERSAL HORROR

After the introduction of sound, Universal's horror films reached screaming pitch with Béla Lugosi's creeping bloodsucker in *Dracula* (1931) and Boris Karloff's human patchwork in *Frankenstein* (1931). Universal were the first studio to make horror films that were designed purely to shock audiences. They produced more tales of the living dead with *The Mummy* (1932) and then had mad scientists on a killing spree in *The Invisible Man* (1933). The gothic set design became a vital part of the chilling atmosphere, particularly in Universal's versions of Edgar Allan Poe's *The Raven* (1935), *The Black Cat* (1934), and *Murders in the rue Morgue* (1932) with their secret dungeons, hidden laboratories, and deathly vaults.

## BORIS KARLOFF

*Boris Karloff became famous when he played the monster in* Frankenstein *(1931). The star of many of Universal's 1930s horror classics, he was a criminal servant in* The Old Dark House *(1932) and* The Raven *(1935), an evil genius in* The Mask of Fu Manchu *(1932), and then a devil-worshipping priest in* The Black Cat *(1934).*

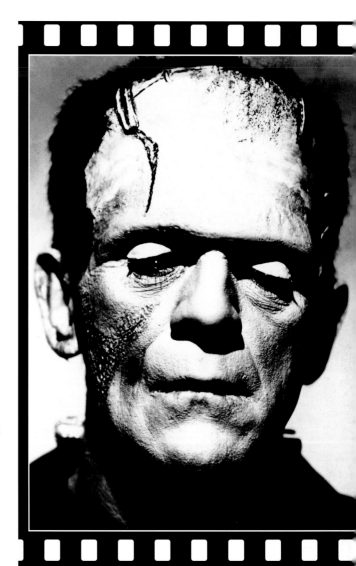

## THE MUMMY'S GHOST (1944)

*The Mummy's Ghost has many of the traditional mummy movie features, including a killer mummy, an Egyptian high priest, and the reincarnation of a mummified queen. This sequel to* The Mummy's Tomb (1942) *is unusual in that the monster does, for once, get the girl.*

# ANCIENT CURSES

When the Egyptian ruler Tutankhamen's tomb was found in 1922, the world was fascinated with stories of mummies and curses. Tales of tombs filled with treasures, secret objects with mystical powers, and mummies coming back to life became popular. The original horror shocker is *The Mummy* (1932), in which the corpse of ancient Egyptian prince, Imhotep, is uncovered, accidentally brought back to life, and let free to go in search of the reincarnation of his lost love. Like *Frankenstein* (1931), *The Mummy* focused on the horror of a corpse coming to life.

## FRANKENSTEIN (1931)

*Dr. Frankenstein, aided by his hunchbacked servant Fritz, steals body parts from fresh graves to create a human being. The creature he gives life to, via a bolt of lightning, becomes a monster when Frankenstein rejects him. With electrodes through his neck and a badly fitting suit, Boris Karloff's monster became the best-known figure in horror.* Frankenstein *has many sequels, including* The Bride of Frankenstein (1935) *which concluded the story of Mary Shelley's novel, where humankind is arrogant enough to believe themselves to be God's equal, and a creator of life.*

## THE MUMMY (1999)

*A mixture of horror, comedy, and adventure, the remake of* The Mummy *tells the story of Imhotep who is resurrected by accident in 1923 by treasure hunters. The walking corpse was created using computer-generated special effects.*

# Vampires

*Based on folk legends and a classic novel by English author Bram Stoker, the screen vampire sleeps in a coffin, wears a cape, has fangs, and speaks with a foreign accent. Vampires can be killed by sunlight and a wooden stake through the heart.*

## The Caped Count

The first screen vampire was the chilling Count Orlok in *Nosferatu, a Symphony of Horror* (1922). German director, Friedrich Murnau found the film's name in Bram Stoker's <u>Dracula</u>, which listed Nosferatu as an ancient word for a vampire. Count Orlok is an eerie creature able to transform himself into wolves and rats. In Dreyer's *Vampyr* (1932), the vampire is also associated with plague and disease when a French village is overrun with vampires. It was *Dracula* (1931) that changed the vampire forever, turning him into a foreign aristocrat, who was both charming and irresistible to his female victims.

### Bela Lugosi

*The man who played Dracula, Béla Lugosi, was born in Transylvania. Unable to speak English, he learned his lines by sound, giving the count his chilling Hungarian accent. Forever famous for his role, Lugosi was buried in the Dracula costume that made him a horror **icon**.*

### Nosferatu, a Symphony of Horror (1922)

*Unable to get the rights to Stoker's <u>Dracula</u>, Murnau created his own vampire, Count Orlok. With rodent teeth and claws, and bat-like ears, the vampire can only be stopped by the sacrifice of a virgin. Count Orlok lacks Dracula's sophistication, but is still able to lure his female victims.*

## BLADE (1998)

*Based on the Marvel comic, Blade is a Dhampir, half-human and half-vampire, after his mother was bitten by a vampire during pregnancy. Blade hunts vampires to avenge his mother's violent death.*

## THE LOST BOYS (1987)

*A vampire version of J. M. Barrie's* Peter Pan, The Lost Boys *is about a group of vampires, who never grow up. Wearing black leather jackets and riding motorbikes, vampires never looked so cool.*

## BLOOD LUST

After he played Count Dracula, Lugosi was a sex symbol, and Hollywood vampires soon left their castles of cobwebs to become glamorous wild boys. In *The Lost Boys* (1987) and *Near Dark* (1987), vampire gangs steal cars and ride motorbikes. *Bram Stoker's Dracula* (1992) is both **gothic** and attractive, as are the lovesick noblemen in *Interview with the Vampire* (1994).

## BRAM STOKER'S DRACULA (1992)

*The closest adaptation of the original novel,* Bram Stoker's Dracula *centres around a young lawyer, Jonathan Harker, who visits a castle in Transylvania to settle a property deal with the deadly Count Dracula. Trapping Harker in his castle, Dracula is inspired by a photo of Jonathan's fiancée Mina as she looks just like his own love, Elisabeta. He goes to London to search for her. Once there, Dracula begins a reign of seduction and terror. Director Francis Ford Coppola's version of the Dracula myth draws on the despair of the vampire, who is haunted by a lost love and is unable to die.*

# ZOMBIES

Zombies are the famous mindless monsters that have haunted the silver screen for decades. Half-rotten corpses rising from the grave to walk the Earth terrorizing humans, zombies have often been used by film makers to comment on society.

## VOODOO ZOMBIES

Originating in an alleged **voodoo** spell to resurrect the dead, the zombie film began with *White Zombie* (1932). Set on the Caribbean island of Haiti, *White Zombie* stars Béla Lugosi as a voodoo master who uses a potion to turn a young bride into a zombie. Another female zombie appears in the chiller *I Walked with a Zombie* (1943) in which a beautiful girl is punished for having an affair, when she is cursed by Caribbean natives, who turn her into a zombie.

### INVASION OF THE BODY SNATCHERS (1956)

*A wave of panic hits America when people are replaced by mindless zombies in* Invasion of the Body Snatchers. *The zombies are monsters intent on destroying humankind, reflecting America's fear of* **communists** *during the* **Cold War**.

### GEORGE A. ROMERO

*Romero wrote, produced, and directed the low budget film,* Night of the Living Dead *(1968), a cult classic for zombie fans. After a few witch and*

*vampire films, Romero again used zombies to comment on society in* Dawn of the Dead *(1978). He completed the 'Dead Trilogy' with* Day of the Dead *(1985).*

### NIGHT OF THE LIVING DEAD (1968)

*Radiation from a fallen satellite causes the dead to rise from their graves and hunt human flesh for food. The humans barricade themselves in a farmhouse to survive the night. The first horror film to have an African-American as its star,* Night of the Living Dead *focuses on race relations.*

## NIGHT OF THE LIVING DEAD (1990)

*In this colour remake of Romero's* Night of the Living Dead, *the story of seven men and women besieged by brain-eating zombies in a remote farmhouse remains the same. However, the heroine is tougher, the zombies more gruesome, and the rescuers more cruel as they hunt down, burn, and torture the zombies.* Night of the Living Dead *was directed by Tom Savini, a master in horror special effects and make-up, who has been creating horrifying creatures for Romero since* Dawn of the Dead. *By twisting the death scenes and the ending, Savini has updated Romero's original to create his own gory shocker.*

## DAWN OF THE DEAD (2004)

*Piling up the shocks, with faster moving, scarier zombies, the* Dawn of the Dead *remake lacks the social criticism of Romero's original, which had zombies wandering mindlessly through shopping malls, just like humans.*

## BACK FROM THE DEAD

Zombies were shown as gruesome killers in *Night of the Living Dead* (1968), where they hunt people for no reason. With the dead rising from their graves, zombie films look at humanity's fight for survival, when society collapses. *Dawn of the Dead* (1978) had shocking visuals of rotting corpses. This grisly horror continued with *Zombi 2* (1979) and *City of the Living Dead* (1980).

## 28 DAYS LATER (2002)

*While not actually zombies, the crazed killers infected with a deadly virus in 28 Days Later show the same relentless determination to harm the living.*

# B-MOVIES

Until the early 1950s, cinemas screened the main feature with a B-movie, a short, cheap film with unknown actors and a formulaic plot. Horror B-movies in the 1950s and 1960s had extra gore, nudity, and violence.

**CAT or WOMAN** or a thing too evil to mention? listen for the SCREAM in the night look into the eyes of the creature who rules the land of the living dead!

Even on her wedding night she must share the man she loved with the 'Female Thing' that lived in the Tomb of the Cat!

AMERICAN INTERNATIONAL presents
EDGAR ALLAN POE'S **TOMB of LIGEIA** COLORSCOPE
VINCENT PRICE and ELIZABETH SHEPHERD
ROBERT TOWNE EDGAR ALLAN POE ROGER CORMAN

## SHLOCK HORROR

In the USA, audiences were freaked out by the new blend of sci-fi and horror. Giant mutant insects terrorized America in *Them!* (1954) and *Attack of the Giant Leeches* (1959), while aliens were the monsters in pulp horrors like *The Attack of the 50-foot Woman* (1958) and *The Blob* (1958). At the same time, the small British company Hammer Films were creating gory horror films, like the creepy *Quatermass Xperiment* (1955), which took advantage of relaxed censorship and the new **X certificate.** Hammer went on a blood fest with remakes of horror classics like *The Curse of Frankenstein* (1957), *Horror of Dracula* (1958), and *The Mummy* (1959).

### TOMB OF LIGEIA (1964)

*The last of Hammer Films' Edgar Allan Poe series, set in creepy **gothic** castles on stormy nights, The Tomb of Ligeia is the tale of a sinister aristocrat, who believes he is being haunted by his dead wife.*

### THE CREATURE FROM THE BLACK LAGOON (1954)

*In this amphibian version of King Kong (1933), the prehistoric 'Gill-Man' is discovered by scientists on the Amazon River. Made by Universal, this sci-fi horror flick with a man in a rubber suit is still considered to be the ultimate monster movie.*

# THE MODERN B-MOVIE

In the 1970s, horror films were less interested in ghost stories and more interested in the taboo subjects of sex and violence, like Hammer's films *The Vampire Lovers* (1970) and *Lust for a Vampire* (1971). The modern B-movie horror is a mixture of extreme violence and a low-budget remake of familiar plots and monsters, such as *The Texas Chainsaw Massacre* (1974) and *The Thing* (1982).

## VINCENT PRICE

*Actor Vincent Price is most famous for his roles in Hammer's series of horrors based on Poe's spooky tales, directed by Roger Corman. He played a torturous madman in* The Pit and the Pendulum *(1961) and a devil-worshipper in* The Masque of the Red Death *(1964).*

## DEEP RISING (1998)

*In this action-packed movie, a strange creature from the deep attacks a gang of thieves on an empty cruise ship. With its A-movie budget,* Deep Rising *is a modern B-movie that delights audiences with a simple plot and stunning special effects, as the monster's tentacles grab victims.*

## THE THING (1982)

*A virtual sequel to* The Thing from Another World *(1951), the film follows a group of American scientists in the Antarctic, as they retrieve the charred body of a dog from a deserted base. When they discover a spaceship, the group realise the dog is in fact a shape-shifting alien, able to change itself into any living thing. As paranoia takes over the group,* The Thing *creates fear out of mutual suspicion, as nobody knows which members of the team are already controlled by the alien.*

# MUTATIONS

*Inspired by ancient legends of werewolf curses and novels of mad scientists unleashing their animal instincts, the screen has often used transformation to horrify audiences.*

## WOLF MEN

Werewolves sprang into film via tribal curses, from Native Americans in *The Werewolf* (1913) and from Tibet in *The Werewolf of London* (1935). After a man is bitten by a werewolf in *The Wolf Man* (1941), he becomes one himself. *The Wolf Man* invented much werewolf mythology, from the transformation from man to werewolf at full moon to killing the wolf with a silver bullet. Comedy horrors *The Howling* (1981) and *An American Werewolf in London* (1981) show the pain of transformation.

### DR JEKYLL AND MR HYDE (1931)

*Based on the novel by Robert Louis Stevenson, Dr Jekyll and Mr Hyde explores human nature as both civilized and animalistic. Transforming into a wolfish monster after taking a potion, the monster Hyde warns against drug abuse and raging desires.*

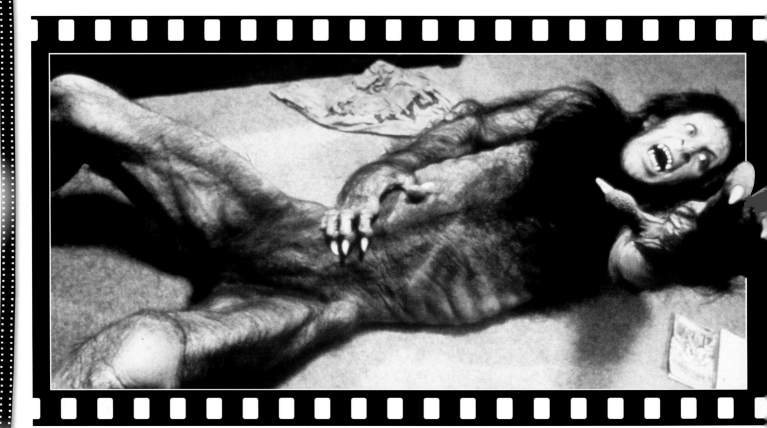

# TRANSFORMATIONS

In *Cat People* (1942) a woman believes she is cursed to become a panther when she is emotional. Men are turned to beasts by mad experiments and nuclear radiation in *The Alligator People* (1959) and *The Slime People* (1963). In *Species* (1995) a beautiful alien-human lures males to mate with her, before she turns into a man-eating monster.

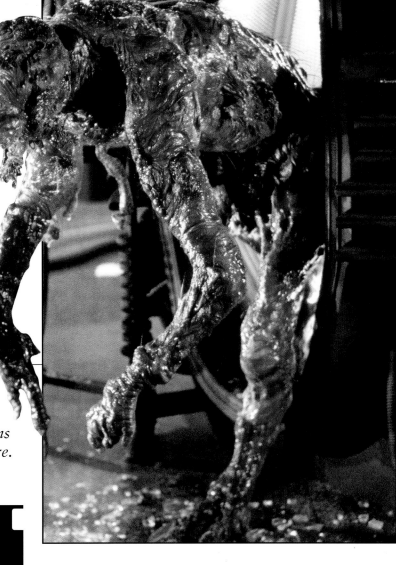

## THE FLY (1986)

*David Cronenberg's gory remake of the 1958 original details a scientist's slow and gruesome transformation from man to fly. With its portrayal of the arrogant scientist,* The Fly *warns of the dangers of interfering with Mother Nature.*

## AN AMERICAN WEREWOLF IN LONDON (1981)

*John Landis' humorous horror focuses on two students who are attacked by a werewolf on the Yorkshire dales. Jack is killed and David is clawed, turning him into a werewolf on the night of the next full moon. Waking up in hospital, David is haunted by nightmares of becoming a werewolf and by visions of Jack's rotting corpse begging him to commit suicide, so that his undead victims can rest in peace. Famed for its painful transformation scene of a man turning into a werewolf,* An American Werewolf in London *won an Oscar for Rick Baker's terrifying special effects. The quirky humour is reinforced by the soundtrack comprised only of songs with the word 'moon' in the title.*

## DAVID CRONENBERG

*Horror and sci-fi director David Cronenberg invented the subgenre of body horror films, these play on human fears of infection and bodily change. Cronenburg shows bodies deformed by disease in* Rabid *(1977) and by watching violent television in* Videodrome *(1983).* eXistenZ *(1999) is based on a **virtual reality** game where the game pod is implanted into the player's spine.*

# DEMONS

*Demons have been portrayed on film under many different guises.*

## THE DEVIL

The devil is traditionally depicted as inhuman, but powerful. In *Häxan* (1922), the devil has ears like bats' wings and claw-like fingers, while in *The Devil Rides Out* (1968) he has the fur, beard, and horns of a goat. The devil looks more human in *Faust* (1926) as Mephistopheles, and in *The Undead* (1957) as Satan. He has even been elegant and suited in *The Sorrows of Satan* (1926) and *Angel on My Shoulder* (1946).

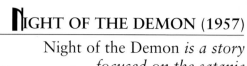

## NIGHT OF THE DEMON (1957)

*Night of the Demon is a story focused on the satanic leader of a devil-worshipping group that manages to horrify with its sinister shadows and monstrous demon from the fires of hell.*

## ANGEL HEART (1987)

*Full of mythological and religious symbols, Angel Heart blends gory horror with the detective story of **film noir**. Lucifer hires a private eye to collect the soul promised to him in a dreadful pact.*

## THE EXORCIST (1973)

*Based on a real life case, The Exorcist tells of Regan, a 12-year-old girl who has symptoms of possession: great strength, the ability to float in the air without support, and to speak foreign languages. Two priests join forces to get rid of the demon inside her. Adapted from the novel by William Peter Blatty, The Exorcist revolutionized the horror film. Its hidden images of painted demons had audiences fainting in the cinema, making it one of the most controversial films ever made.*

### ROSEMARY'S BABY (1968)

*Rosemary is selected to bear the enemy of Christ's child when her husband makes a pact with their devil-worshipping neighbours. In* Rosemary's Baby *the Devil is a hideous beast with hair and claws.*

# CULTS AND COVENS

Some films focus on the Devil's attempt to enter the world. In *The Black Cat* (1934) and *The Seventh Victim* (1943), young women are the victims of devil-worshipping cults. The satanic cult in *The Wicker Man* (1973) sacrifices a young woman to honour their god. In *Blood on Satan's Claw* (1970), young children turn into devil-worshippers when Satan's bodily remains are dug up. Children and babies also become the Devil's door into the human world in *The Omen* (1976) and *Rosemary's Baby* (1968), when mothers give birth to Satan's children.

### SAM RAIMI

*Sam Raimi's debut, low-budget feature* The Evil Dead *(1981) became a cult hit due to its mix of black comedy and extreme violence. When ancient demons threaten and possess five friends in an isolated cabin in the woods, their fight for survival becomes a gory splatter fest. With body parts flying,* The Evil Dead II *(1987) is usually viewed as a comedy remake.*

### ARMY OF DARKNESS (1993)

*More a comedy than a horror film, the final part of the* Evil Dead *trilogy of three films features Ash, the sole survivor of the two earlier movies. He is armed with a chainsaw against the undead and an army of skeletons, led by his evil double.*

# Phantoms

*Set in isolated mansions on stormy nights, ghost chillers in haunted houses have become a film genre in their own right. With boarded-up rooms, sliding wall panels and secret passageways, guests spend a night battling the house for survival.*

## The Old Dark House

With its creepy shadows and cobweb-covered mansion, *The Cat and the Canary* (1927) introduced many hallmarks of the haunted house style, including hidden panels and hands coming out of walls. Often lured to creepy houses to inherit money or escape thunderstorms, guests also suffer rattling doorknobs and a murderous manservant in *Night of Terror* (1933) and *The Old Dark House* (1932).

While the ghostly frights are usually devised by humans, *The Haunting* (1963) shows a vengeful spirit that is the result of repeated violence and tragedy in the house.

### House on Haunted Hill (1959)

*Guests at a haunted house party, thrown by an eccentric millionaire and his scheming wife, are spooked out of their wits by decapitated heads, walking skeletons, and falling chandeliers in William Castle's old dark house classic House on Haunted Hill.*

### Japanese Horror

*With deadly videotapes and ghost children, Japanese horror films reveal a modern world infected by spirits seeking revenge. Ringu (1998) and Dark Water (2002) both show women investigating the deaths of abused children to save their own families.*

## THE SIXTH SENSE (1999)

*This spooky chiller is centred around a young boy who sees the ghosts of dead people, and the psychologist who tries to help him. Unravelling the mystery of spirits who don't realize they're dead, The Sixth Sense is a ghost story thriller with a twist.*

## POLTERGEIST (1982)

*Rather than the restless spirits of the dead, Tobe Hooper's Poltergeist used modern technology to terrorize, when a young girl starts communicating with ghosts through the television.*

## SPOOKED

As audiences got used to the haunted house horrors, the makers of ghost films had to invent new ways of scaring them. Based on Henry James' novel <u>The Turn of the Screw,</u> The Innocents (1961) tells of children possessed by the spirits of dead servants. A father is driven to madness and murder when he works as a caretaker in a haunted hotel in *The Shining* (1980), while *The Fog* (1980) shows ghosts seeking revenge.

## THE OTHERS (2001)

*Set in a crumbling mansion on the foggy island of Jersey at the end of World War II, The Others focuses on Grace and her two children, who suffer from an allergy to sunlight. Despite their obsessive door-locking, the family begin to realize that their home might be haunted. Inspired by Henry James'* <u>The Turn of the Screw,</u> *The Others is a return to the well-crafted ghost story, terrifying at every turn.*

# CRITTERS

*Spawned by man's phobia of bugs, bees, and birds, the animals-run-amok horror movie sees nature, overrun by pollution and nuclear radiation, take revenge against humankind.*

## NASTY NATURE

With crazed flapping and savage pecking, Alfred Hitchcock's *The Birds* (1963) launched the nature-gone-mad movie. In *Frogs* (1972) it is mutant reptiles and amphibians that attack humankind, while bears are on the prowl in *Grizzly* (1976). A family is mauled by man's best friend in *Cujo* (1983), when a pet dog becomes infected with the disease rabies. *Jaws* (1975) turned the oceans into a fear zone forever, and schools of flesh-hungry fish followed in *Piranha* (1978), *Orca* (1977), and the shark-infested *Open Water* (2003).

"It could be the most terrifying motion picture I have ever made!"

PLEASE DO NOT [...] THE END FIRST
See it from the begin[...]

ALFRE[D] HITCHCOCK "The Birds"
TECHNICOLOR
Based on Daphne Du Maurier's classic suspense story!

STARRING ROD TAYLOR · JESSICA TANDY · SUZANNE PLESHETTE and introducing 'TIPPI' HEDREN
Screenplay by EVAN HUNTER · Directed by ALFRED HITCHCOCK

### THE BIRDS (1963)

*Flocks of crows and seagulls peck at children and gouge out people's eyes. Pollution and atomic power are possible explanations, but the real horror lies in the random nature of the attacks.*

### GRIZZLY (1976)

*The success of* Jaws *(1975) inspired many beast horror films, including the gruesome Grizzly, which had an 18-foot bear attacking campers in a national park.*

## ALIENS (1986)

*In James Cameron's* Aliens *the colony planet LV426 is overrun with aliens. In order to save a little girl and other planets from the slime-oozing monsters and their egg-laying alien queen, LV426 has to be blown up.*

## INSECTS ATTACK!

The killer bug movie was hatched in the 1950s, as a result of America's fears about atomic power. Giant mutant ants are spawned in *Them!* (1954), while toxic cockroaches set fire to their victims in *Bug* (1975), and chomp their way through humans in *The Nest* (1988). Plagues of South American killer bees terrorise in *The Bees* (1978) and *The Swarm* (1978), when the delicate balance of nature is upset. Horror also made use of spiders in *Tarantula* (1955), with mammoth, man-eating spiders on the prowl, and famously in *Arachnophobia* (1990), when spiders invade the USA.

## JAWS (1975)

*Based on Peter Benchley's novel, director Steven Spielberg's film,* Jaws, *fills the beach with fear, as holiday-making teenagers are picked off by a great white shark lurking beneath the surface. Winning an Academy Award™ for John Williams' spine-chilling musical score,* Jaws *is a horror film filled with suspense. While shocking audiences with decapitated heads and sudden attacks by the killer, the film's greatest terror comes from not seeing the shark. In fact, the role of the mechanical shark was greatly reduced during filming, when it kept breaking down.*

## H. R. GIGER

*Hans Rüdi Giger is a Swiss painter and designer, most famous for his work on Ridley Scott's* Alien *(1979). Based on his own painting* Necronom V, *Giger created the Oscar™ Award winning design for the alien, monstrously combining mechanical and natural elements.*

# SERIAL KILLERS

*Unlike the supernatural origins of other horror films, the **serial killer** movie gets its sinister chill by being part of the real world. Serial murderers like Jack the Ripper and Ed Gein are both terrifying and fascinating, inspiring filmmakers to create films which force society to confront its real fears.*

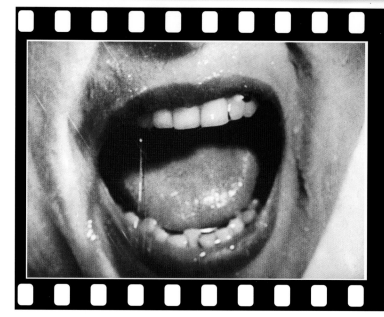

## ED GEIN

*The murders of serial killer Ed Gein inspired many horror films, including* Psycho *(1960),* The Texas Chainsaw Massacre *(1974), and* In the Light of the Moon *(2000). After mutilating the bodies of female corpses, taken from graves, Gein descended into murder and cannibalism.*

## PSYCHO MURDERERS

Loosely based on the Jack the Ripper legend, Alfred Hitchcock's *The Lodger* (1926) injects a fog-choked London with terror, as a killer lurks behind every corner. While Hitchcock's murderer chooses blonde women as his victims, in *M* (1931) the deranged killer picks on children. Fritz Lang's *M* focuses on the psychology of the deranged child-killer, who struggles against his murderous impulse, but cannot help himself. Mentally disturbed due to childhood experiments by his father, the murderer in *Peeping Tom* (1960) uses a camera to film the terror on his victims' faces as he kills them.

## HENRY: PORTRAIT OF A SERIAL KILLER (1986)

*Based on murderer Henry Lee Lucas, this low-budget film is disturbingly realistic. With its depiction of violent murders,* Henry: Portrait of a Serial Killer *horrifies and repulses the viewer, forcing them to question the morality of watching extremely violent movies.*

## PSYCHO (1960)

*Adapted from the novel by Robert Bloch, which drew on the crimes of Ed Gein, Psycho tells the story of petty thief Marion Crane, who steals $40,000 from her boss to start a new life with boyfriend Sam. On route to California, she stops at the Bates Motel, where she meets timid Norman and his psychopathic mother. With a publicity stunt to protect the killer's identity, Psycho changed screen history forever, no longer allowing entry to the cinema mid-film, but forcing moviegoers to see the film from the beginning.*

### SILENCE OF THE LAMBS (1991)

*When he played 'Hannibal the Cannibal', Anthony Hopkins created a terrifying screen killer. Things go wrong when the police use Hannibal to help capture a serial killer.*

# KILLING SPREES

Modern serial killer movies, like *The Boston Strangler* (1968) or *Badlands* (1973), have dramatized the lives of real-life murderers. Other films question the media's portrayal of violence. *Natural Born Killers* (1994) turns killers into superstars overnight, while *Man Bites Dog* (1992) has a camera crew who become accomplices in the murders they are filming. Films like *Se7en* (1995) and *American Psycho* (2000) use serial murders to examine society's superficial obsession with appearance, pleasure, and greed.

### COPYCAT (1995)

*In this cop-versus-killer thriller, a murderer is on the loose. The killer's crimes are imitations of real murders, committed by the notorious serial killers Ted Bundy, Jeffrey Dahmer, and the Boston Strangler.*

# THE SLASHER MOVIE

T Still reeling from a spate of serial murders, the United States confronted its fears in the stalk-and-slash horror, where teenagers are under threat from a deranged killer who just keeps coming.

## TEXAS CHAINSAW MASSACRE (1974)

*Inspired by real-life serial murderer, Ed Gein, the chainsaw-wielding killer in this film wears a creepy leather mask and eats humans. Realistic camerawork helps to make* The Texas Chainsaw Massacre's *'Leatherface' a truly terrifying killer.*

## STALK AND SLASH

The slasher movie grew from **serial killer** thrillers, like *Psycho* (1960) and *Peeping Tom* (1960). The stalk-and-slash horror began with *The Texas Chainsaw Massacre* (1974), *Black Christmas* (1974), and *Halloween* (1978), which used crazed killers, rather than blood and gore, to generate terror. Mind games continued in *Friday the 13th* (1980), when teenagers are murdered for reopening Camp Crystal Lake, where a young boy drowned years before.

## HALLOWEEN (1978)

*Shot on a budget of just $300,000,* Halloween *brought the evil killer from the wilderness into the suburban home. With a mentally disturbed masked killer stalking an innocent heroine,* Halloween *set the standards for the slasher movie, inspiring many gorier imitations.*

## A NIGHTMARE ON ELM STREET (1984)

*Wes Craven added a twist to the stalk-and-slash formula by creating a killer who inhabits children's dreams when they fall asleep. Having nightmares of a scarred serial killer with knives for fingers, the teenagers of Elm Street have to stay awake to stay alive. With its bizarre psycho Freddy Krueger, who never seems to be quite dead,* A Nightmare on Elm Street *gives a chilling portrait of the suburbs, where a child killer is burnt to death by parents and neighbours.*

## WES CRAVEN

*Beginning his career as a university professor and part-time editor, Wes Craven shot to fame with his cult classic* Last House on the Left *(1972), which he wrote, edited, and directed. His interest in horror took a supernatural twist in* The Hills Have Eyes *(1977) which is about a family stranded in the desert and stalked by killers*

## SCREAM 2 (1997)

*Expanding on the clever references to slasher classics in Scream (1996), Scream 2 provides a similar mix of laughs, frights, and twists.*

## RULES OF THE GAME

With an endless number of films, the slasher movie established a formula, with varying amounts of comedy and gore. The formulaic battle between the innocent teenage girl and the murderer has been the focus of horror comedies like the *Scream* trilogy (1996, 1997 & 2000), which pokes fun at the stalk-and-slash rules. The comic slasher *Scary Movie* (2000) makes fun of modern horror films from *I Know What You Did Last Summer* (1997) to *The Blair Witch Project* (1999).

# HORROR RE-INVENTED

## LITTLE SHOP OF HORRORS (1960)

*Shot in two days with a budget of just $27,000 The Little Shop of Horrors is a horror comedy that follows a florist's assistant, who is persuaded into supplying his new friend, a meat-eating talking plant, with increasing amounts of human flesh for dinner.*

*A finely balanced mix of humour and splatter, the horror comedy spread from the haunted house spoof,* The Ghost Breakers *(1940) to the comedian and monster revival in* Abbott and Costello Meet Frankenstein *(1948).*

## HORROR COMEDY

Roger Corman's cult movies *The Little Shop of Horrors* (1960) and *A Bucket of Blood* (1959) blend together gory horror and black comedy to satirize modern life. The clumsy vampire slayers in *Dance of the Vampires* (1967) and the moronic zombies in *Shaun of the Dead* (2004) make fun of the horror genre, while *Battle Royale* (2000) uses comic-strip violence to poke fun at reality television shows.

## TIM BURTON

*Director Tim Burton used his unique style to inject ghosts and monsters into suburban life in* Beetle Juice *(1988) and* Edward Scissorhands *(1991). His film* The Nightmare before Christmas *(1993) is a fantastic blend of horror, comedy, musical and animation.*

## BEETLE JUICE (1988)

*A haunted house movie with a comic twist, Beetle Juice is the story of two recently deceased newlyweds, who have asked Betelgeuse, a 'bio-exorcist', to get rid of the mortals who have taken over their home. Beetle Juice is a dark, hilarious horror film.*

*Pieced together from footage supposedly found in the Black Hills Forest,* The Blair Witch Project *follows three film students making a documentary about the Blair witch legend. Filming their experiences, the three students are terrorized by an unseen figure. Costing only $22,000 to produce and making $240 million at the box-office, this film terrified audiences with its intense internet campaign, designed to convince people that the footage was real.*

# HAIR-RAISING REMAKES

As cinematic technology improves, Hollywood studios seek to scare with remakes of horror classics. B-movies from the 1950s, including *The Blob* (1958) and *The Fly* (1958), have been remade with improved special effects, while *Bram Stoker's Dracula* (1992) and *Mary Shelley's Frankenstein* (1994) have returned to the original novels for inspiration. Successful Japanese chillers, like *Ringu* (1998), *Dark Water* (2002) and *Ju-on: The Grudge* (2003), have been remade for American audiences, and remakes of *The Texas Chainsaw Massacre* (2003) and *Dawn of the Dead* (2004) have replaced bloodcurdling terror with more violence and gore.

## MARY SHELLEY'S FRANKENSTEIN (1994)

*Returning to the 1818 novel,* Mary Shelley's Frankenstein *bypassed Universal's bolt-necked horror icon, replacing horror thrills with a dark story of creation. Highlighting the tragedy of the rejected monster, the film explores the human in the monster, and the monster in the human.*

## THE RING (2002)

*Gore Verbinski's remake of Hideo Nakata's* Ringu *(1998) tells the story of a female journalist racing against time to investigate a cursed videotape, which kills those who watch it seven days later.*

# FILM TECHNOLOGY

## TRADITIONAL MAKE-UP

'The Man of a Thousand Faces' Lon Chaney had to be creative with his monster make-up for The Hunchback of Notre Dame (1923). He used a curly wig, false teeth, a glass eye, and a plaster hump to play Quasimodo. Jack Pierce created the monster in Frankenstein (1931) by using layers of rubber and cotton to extend Karloff's forehead. Karloff took out his false teeth to make his cheeks more sunken

and wore green greasepaint to look like a corpse. Make-up genius Dick Smith, who created the head-spinning, vomiting demon in The Exorcist (1973), developed latex moulds, which have been used for horror monsters, like Dawn of the Dead (1978), ever since.

## CGI MAKE-UP

The skeletal ghosts in Pirates of the Caribbean: Curse of the Black Pearl (2003) were brought to life by special effects company Industrial Light & Magic. To make the corpses, a digital skeleton was created that fitted each character according to 3D body scans of the actors. Layers were then added to the skeletons. These layers included skin, which was based on scanned turkey meat, hair, and clothing. The clothing could then be digitally altered using different textures, folds, and shadows.

# GLOSSARY

**Cold War**

state of hostility between nations without an actual war. The term usually describes the situation between the Soviet Union and the USA between 1945 and 1991.

**communism**

political theory that class should be abolished and all land and wealth that a country has, shared out equally

**film noir**

film genre associated with violence and crime. Films are often set in the darkness of night with rainy streets.

**German expressionism**

style of art, music or writing, particularly of the 1900s, which shows people's states of mind

**gothic**

style of art and writing that was popular in the eighteenth and nineteenth centuries, usually used to describe something very gloomy or horrifying

**icon**

person or thing seen as a symbol, and held up as something sacred or an example to be followed

**psychological**

having to do with the mind, or relating to the scientific study of the mind and the way it works

**serial killer**

person who murders more than three victims one at a time in a relatively short period of time

**silent film**

film without any sound

**slasher films**

horror movies in which people are killed very violently with knives

**virtual reality**

set of images and sounds produced by a computer to represent a place or situation that someone can experience

**voodoo**

practice of, or belief in, religious witchcraft, mainly found in the West Indies and southern USA

**X certificate**

the first film classification set by the British Board of Film Censors (BBFC), to give an age restriction of 16 to certain films

# INDEX

## FILM TITLES INDEX